Merry Xmas! A.S.

CARICATURE OF TO-DAY Yesterday

*Printed and Engraved in Great Britain
by Herbert Reiach Ltd., 43 Belvedere
Road. London. S.E. 1.
Offset plates by Vincent Brooks Day
and Son, Ltd., London.*

WILLIAM HOGARTH

Design'd & Engrav'd by W. Hogarth.

The BENCH.

Publish'd as the Act directs. 4 Sep. 1758.

Of the different meaning of the Words Character, Caracatura and Outrè in Painting and Drawing.

There are hardly any two things more essentially different than Character and Caracatura, nevertheless they are usually confounded and mistaken for each other: on which account this Explanation is attempted. It has ever been allow'd that, when a Character is strongly mark'd in the living Face, it may be consider'd as an Index of the mind, to express which with any degree of justness in Painting, requires the utmost Efforts of a great Master. Now that which has, of late Years, got the name of Caracatura, is, or ought to be totally divested of every Stroke that hath a tendency to good Drawing: it may be said to be a Species of Lines that are produc'd rather by the hand of chance than of Skill; for the early Scrawlings of a Child which do but barely hint an Idea of an Human Face, will always be found to be like some Person or other, and will often form such a Comical Resemblance as in all probability the most eminent Caracaturers of these times will not be able to equal with Design, because their Ideas of Objects are so much more perfect than Childrens, that they will unavoidably introduce some kind of Drawing: for all the humourous Effects of the fashionable manner of Caracaturing chiefly depend on the surprize we are under at finding our selves caught with any sort of Similitude in objects absolutely remote in their kind. Let it be observ'd the more remote in their Nature the greater is the Excellence of these Pieces; as a proof of this, I remember a famous Caracatura of a certain Italian Singer, that struck at first sight, which consisted only of a Streight perpendicular Stroke with a Dot over it. As to the French word Outrè it is different from the foregoing, and signifies nothing more than the exagerated outlines of a Figure, all the parts of which may be in other respects a perfect and true Picture of Nature. A Giant or a Dwarf may be call'd a common Man Outrè. So any part as a Nose, or a Leg, made bigger or less than it ought to be, is that part Outrè, † which is all that is to be understood by this word, so injudiciously us'd to the prejudice of Character. ——— See Excess Analysis of Beauty. Chap. 6.

⁂ The unfinish'd Groupe of Heads in the upper part of this Print was added by the Author in Octr 1764: & was intended as a further Illustration of what is here said concerning Character Caracatura & Outrè, He worked upon it the Day before his Death which happened the 26th of that Month.

"THE BENCH"

CARICATURE OF TO-DAY

With an Introduction by
Randall Davies, F.S.A.

1928
EDITED BY GEOFFREY HOLME
THE STUDIO LTD., 44 LEICESTER SQ., LONDON, W.C.2

CONTENTS

Page

" On Caricature," by Randall Davies, F.S.A. 1

ILLUSTRATIONS
Caricaturists

Plate

d'Ache, Caran 22, 23
Agi 136
Andersen, Ryszard 52
Arnold, Karl 126
Auerbach-Levy, William 90, 91

Barton, Ralph 113, 114, 115
Bateman, H. M. 32, 33, 34
Bawden, Edward 88
Baxter, W. G. 14
Beaton, Cecil 68, 69
Beerbohm, Max 78
Berger, Oscar 101, 102
Bib 131
Binder, Pearl 76
Blanco 125
Bofa, Gus 79, 129
Bosse, Abraham 3
Busch, Wilhelm 11

Callot, Jacques 1
Cham 21
Cheney, Leo 110
Cocteau, Jean 116, 117
Covarrubias, Miguel 120, 121
Cruikshank, George 9

Daumier, Honoré 7
Doyle, Richard 10
Dubout 133
Dulac, Edmund 63, 64, 65
Dyson, Will 38

Echea, Enrique 99, 100
Eighteenth-century artist 2
Eliseev, K. 112
Evans, Powys 105, 106, 107, 108, 109

Faivre, Abel 86
Fish 72, 73
Fraser, Eric 94

	Plate
Frueh, Alfred	123, 124
Furniss, Harry	27
Gal	80
Garetto, Paolo	136
Gavarni	17
Gec	136
Girus	136
Gropper, William	134
Gulbransson, Olaf	43, 44
Hahmann, Werner	70, 71
Hammond, Aubrey	104
Heath, H.	6
Heine, Th. Th.	30
Hogarth, William	Frontispiece
Hokusai	8
House, James, Jr.	122
Hynes	74
Johnson, Arthur	87
Johnson, Herbert	75
Kapp	60, 61, 62
Keimel	132
Kyosai	34
Léandre, Charles	28, 29
Lear, Edward	12
Low	81, 82, 83, 85
Lynch, Bohun	89
McLaren, Jack	103
Martin, Charles	128
Matt	95, 96
May, Phil	15, 16
Nerman	97, 98
Oberländer, Adolf	42
Paul Bruno	36, 37
Paul, Hermann	25, 26
Poy	45
Ravilious, Eric	35
Reg	127
Robinson, W. Heath	54
Rodo, L.	55

		Plate
Rouveyre, André	. . . .	56, 57, 58, 59
Rowlandson, Thomas	. . . .	4, 5
Sama	. . . .	111
Sava	. . . .	92, 93
Schilling, E.	. . . .	49
Sem	. . . .	46
Shepherd, J. A.	. . . .	24
Spy	. . . .	18, 19
Stout, Loren	. . . .	130
Tell	. . . .	50
Tenniel, John	. . . .	13
Thomson, A. R.	. . . .	51
Thöny, E.	. . . .	48
Titt, Tom	. . . .	118, 119
Tonks, Henry	. . . .	31
Toulouse-Lautrec, Henri de	. . . .	20
Trilussa	. . . .	136
Vinci, Leonardo de	. . . .	I
Watts, Arthur	. . . .	66, 67
Whitelaw, George	. . . .	53
Wilke, Rudolf	. . . .	39, 40, 41
Williams, Gluyas	. . . .	135
Wilson, David	. . . .	77
Zinkeisen, Doris	. . . .	47

Subjects

		Plate
Abendempfang	. . . .	126
Academy, The	. . . .	5
Academy, The Royal	. . . .	38
Ally Sloper	. . . .	14
Animal Spirits	. . . .	24
d'Annunzio, Gabriele	. . . .	44
Arte Dramatico	. . . .	99
Avocats, deux	. . . .	7
Avory, The Hon. Mr. Justice	. . . . . .	61
Bakst, Léon	. . . .	63
Barrès, Maurice	. . . .	58
Belloc, Hilaire	. . . .	85
Bench, The	. . . .	Frontispiece
Bennett, Arnold	. . . .	77
Bennett, Sir Henry Curtis	. . . .	108
Bernhardt, Sarah	. . . .	56

								Plate
Berry, W. H.	.	.	.	.	.	.	.	119
Bourget, Paul	.	.	.	.	.	.	.	57
Boy on a Rustic Seat	.	.	.	.	.	.	.	35
Brandes, Georg	.	.	.	.	.	.	.	43
Briand, M.	.	.	.	.	.	.	.	131
Bridge Problem	.	.	.	.	.	.	.	127
British Theatre, The	.	.	.	.	.	.	.	83
Brown, Teddy	.	.	.	.	.	.	.	72
Bureaucrat	.	.	.	.	.	.	.	112
Caricature Scrap Book	.	.	.	.	.	.	.	6
Caroline, Queen	.	.	.	.	.	.	.	2
Cecil, Lord Robert	.	.	.	.	.	.	.	89
Cézanne, Paul	.	.	.	.	.	.	.	115
Chamberlain, The Rt. Hon. Sir Austen	.	.	.	.	48, 93, 131	
Chanson Triste	.	.	.	.	.	.	.	66
Cinema Celebrities	.	.	.	.	.	113, 114	
Claire, Ina	.	.	.	.	.	.	.	124
Clarkson, Willy	.	.	.	.	.	.	.	74
Clémenceau, M.	.	.	.	.	.	.	.	29
Cocido a la Espagnola	.	.	.	.	.	.	.	99
Collier, Constance	.	.	.	.	.	.	.	124
Collins, José	.	.	.	.	.	.	.	98
Conservatocialists, The	.	.	.	.	.	.	.	82
Cooper, The Lady Diana	.	.	.	.	.	.	.	69
Cuban Cabinet, The	.	.	.	.	.	.	.	125
Darwin, Charles	.	.	.	.	.	.	.	18
Degas, Edgar	.	.	.	.	.	.	.	115
Delysia	.	.	.	.	.	.	.	97
Derby, The	.	.	.	.	.	.	.	9
Detective, Study of a	.	.	.	.	.	.	.	67
Dilly and Dally	.	.	.	.	.	.	.	45
Doyle, Sir Arthur Conan	.	.	.	.	.	.	.	92
Drumont, M. E.	.	.	.	.	.	.	.	28
Early Queuers, The	.	.	.	.	.	.	.	54
Enfant Terrible, Das	.	.	.	.	.	.	.	87
English Civilisation	.	.	.	.	.	.	.	37
Etiquette for America	.	.	.	.	.	.	.	75
Farrar, Gwen	.	.	.	.	.	.	.	118
Fashion Model, The	.	.	.	.	.	.	.	130
Fashionable Worlde, Ye	.	.	.	.	.	.	.	10
Fitz, of Ciro's	.	.	.	.	.	.	.	104
Fracasse, le Capitaine	.	.	.	.	.	.	.	3
France, Anatole	.	.	.	.	.	.	.	59
Froude, James Anthony	.	.	.	.	.	.	.	19
Fry, Roger	.	.	.	.	.	.	31, 109	
Gauguin, Paul	.	.	.	.	.	.	.	115

	Plate
German Clerical Life	30
Gerz, Valeska	102
Government Gus	45
Grock	50
Grotesque Heads	1
Guedalla, Philip	104
Guilbert, Yvette	20
Haldane, Lord	60
Hale, Binnie	68
Harris, Jed	91
Harvey, Colonel George	106
Hindenburg, Field-Marshal	49
Hippopotamus, The	132
Höhere Lakaien	41
Holmes, Sir Charles	107
Hotei	8
Italy, In the public eye in	136
Jazz Band	47
King, Cecil	33
Knoblock, Edward	77
Koval, M.	128
Kreisler, Fritz	122
Lark, Kingsley	98
Lenihan Winifred	123
Levrette de Madame la Duchesse	22
Little Moritz's Scribbling Book	42
Long Story, A	135
Loos, Anita	73
Macdonald, Ramsay	110
Manet, Edouard	115
Marionettes	88
Matisse, Henri	115
Members of Parliament	27
Mendès, Catulle	58
Metropolitan Police	55
Millerand, M.	117
Ministre, Monsieur le	86
Montesquion, Comte Robert de	57
Moore, George	65
Murger, Henry	79
Musica, Arte, Café y Literatura	100
Mussolini, Signor	70, 134
Negro Head	120
Nonsense, The Book of	12

	Plate
Old Favourite, An	84
O'Neill, Eugene	90
Oracles, The	81
Otero, La Belle	25
Pavlova, Anna	101
Piano Player	13
Picasso, Pablo	115
Poincaré, M.	71, 87, 95
Pollock, Sir Ernest	62
Polyte dans le Grand Monde	23
Premier, The	96
Président de la République	116
Punch Bowl, The	4
Radio Improvements	94
Renard, Jules	129
Renoir, Auguste	115
Réunon Electorale	26
Rothschild, James de	46
Rothschild, Maurice de	46
Sadleir, Michael	104
Salon, The	17
Shaw, George Bernard	64
Sistine Madonna, Before the	39, 40
Sitwell, Mr. Osbert and Mr. Sacheverell	78
Smith, Aubrey	121
So Likely !	15
Sorel, Cécile	59
Springtime Pursuits	34
Stresemann, Herr	52, 131
Tate, Harry	53
Thomassin the engraver	1
Tonks, Professor Henry	105
Uncle Thomas's Cabinet	82
Walker, June	121
Warum ?	36
Webb, Sydney	80
Whitechapel : Saturday Morning	16
Wife of an Important Person	76
Willingdon, Viscount	103
Wood, Derwent	32
Zangwill, Israel	51
Zelli, Joe	104

FOREWORD

This is an age which in spite of its standardisation is full of extraordinary personalities. We need take only two examples and quote Bernard Shaw and Mussolini—the supermen respectively of politics and letters. They are an inspiration to the caricaturist and make noble formulæ for the exaggerated draughtsmanship which flourishes to-day. The oddity of an outline, the expressive capacity of blank space, the rich suggestion of a drawing that is incomplete, the humour and satire that are born of an economical use of materials, are exploited now more than ever before. Caricature, like poetry, is a criticism of life, and as this is a highly critical period, so caricature is correspondingly acute. We have always one means of coping with the fantastic events and characters which dominate modern life—we can be amused. A smile is better than a revolution and the pencil much more convenient than the sword.

There is a tradition, it goes without saying, out of which the modern caricature has developed. We illustrate the tradition in this book the better to show the point we have reached : while Mr. Randall Davies in his introduction brings us to the threshold of to-day and then with an epigram bids us adieu, wisely leaving the present generation to speak for itself.

Every age, of course, has extraordinary personalities and also a sense of the ridiculous. Achilles would have been intolerable without his heel, and Mr. Gladstone had his collars just as Mr. Thomas has his dress-shirt. But each age varies. The coarse laughter of the Georgians, the refined joviality of the Victorians, the somewhat faded elegance of the 'nineties, are replaced by the incisive and self-possessed mockery of to-day.

The editor has received from all over the world vast packages of drawings and of the periodicals which keep alight the lamp of satire. Both editors and artists have lent generous assistance to make the book a complete picture of the caricature of the modern age. The editor wishes to express his great appreciation to all those who contributed material and also his apologies to those whose work was crowded out for lack of space and to those who, for the same reason, have not been represented as fully as he could have wished.

ON CARICATURE

BY a merciful dispensation of Providence, the Italian word *caricatura* was imported into England early in the eighteenth century, and became so thoroughly acclimatised that when it was wafted across the channel in its French form, as *caricature*, late in the eighteenth, there was no excuse for the fabrication of a new one. But for this very fortunate circumstance, the title of the present volume would, no doubt, have had to be " Gelœography," under the terms of the Legacy of Greece. A Cartoon in the Athenian newspapers to-day is labelled (where there is any possibility of a misunderstanding) Γελοιογραφια for Epicurean and Stoic readers alike.

Not but what the two things are radically different in origin. The one word simply means loading on to a car, the other a laughter picture—grin-cut as perhaps it may, one of these days, be called in America. *Caricatura* started as a quite ordinary word, but gradually acquired secondary meanings—always a dangerous thing for a respectable word—among which was the loading of a ship, a gun and (by obvious analogy) a sausage. It also meant an overloading or exaggeration, which has usually been held to explain its employment in connection with our subject ; but the similar association of the word " farce " with the idea of charging or stuffing a dull subject or substance with something spicy and tasty, suggests that the former is the true explanation of so common-place a word being used for " a ridiculous portrait in which the defects are exaggerated," as the term is defined in the modern Italian encyclopædia. Exaggeration is certainly a factor in making the dull portrait funny, but it is not the determining one, which—as in the case of brandied cherries—is rather the spirit with which it is permeated.

Caricatura, again, was a term applied simply to portraits, and to this day this meaning is the first that occurs to the mind in connection with " a caricature." It is only of late years that, as a general term, " caricature " has come to embrace every sort of " laughter picture " or pictorial or political satire. This extension of the term was by no means sudden, arbitrary or unwarranted, and the history of its empire would fill a very much larger and more curious book than the present volume ; but for the present the derivation of the term itself and its primary application will be enough to show us the real nature of the subject, which is apt to be lost sight of amid the profusion of variegated efflorescence which has overgrown it, not always without considerable addition of attraction.

It is a little disheartening to find that the roots of caricature are personal peculiarities, physical defects, and that to bring the plant to maturity is to exaggerate them. But it is none the less interesting to observe the subtleties practised by its cultivators, in the light of this knowledge of what lies below, of the nature of the plant, and to see how exaggeration is subordinated to higher processes until, as in the case of Gavarni or Du Maurier, it is hardly perceptible even as a flavour. But there it is ; the essence of caricature is the exaggeration or at least the accentuation of physical peculiarities, and the success of it, alas, is not due to a general inclination to laughter common to the human race, but to a particular sense of amusement at the unfortunate personal characteristics of one's fellow creatures. " Man has laughed," says Champfleury in his efforts to recover the lost traces of caricature in days of antiquity, " Man has laughed, as he has wept, in every age " ; very likely he has, whether he was laughing at a caricature or at something quite different. But Champfleury might have adduced with more point the ribald outcry that incensed Elisha—" Go up, thou bald head ! " Caricature is, first of all, an attack on a man's appearance, and when that yields it is usually accompanied into ruin by his dignity, and the rest follows according to the circumstances of the case. From the very earliest ages human beings have been very touchy about their personal appearance, and even the gods found amusement in the limping gait of Vulcan ; so that as soon as the artists began to employ their talents for graphic representation of any peculiar features of their enemies, or even of their friends and acquaintances, they were entering on a very wide and very fertile field of operations.

To what extent they availed themselves of their opportunities in the distant past it is rather difficult to say, because such work would have been essentially ephemeral and only have survived its author and its subject by the merest chance. But there is no certain trace of anything of the sort in European painting before the sixteenth century, and Leonardo expressly mentions that the grotesque heads he drew were from exact observation of life.

It was in the School of the Carracci that *caricatura* was born, and it attained a lusty adolescence during the seventeenth century under the fostering influence of their pupils and followers in Bologna and other Italian cities. Count Malaguzzi has outlined the story of this early development in a recent publication, " L'Arte Gaia," but he only indicates the sources from which it may be fully set forth, as no doubt it will have to be, sooner or later.

Caricatura was known in England quite early in the eighteenth century, although at that date " the Grand Tour " was probably rarer for the English than in later years ; but the number of Italian visitors to this country was swelled by the arrival of opera singers in considerable numbers, and it is quite probable that they helped to acclimatise both the word and the practice of caricatura. " The Landing of Senesino " is the subject of one of the earliest of the English examples and there are others of Cuzzoni and of Handel himself, who was chiefly responsible for the Italian invasion. Captain Marcellus Laroon, who drew social subjects, most of which may be dated before 1735, has left a drawing which is inscribed " Matthew Ashton, the Painter, a Caricatura." Peter Tillemans etched a head of Nunez, a Jew picture dealer mentioned by Laroon, entitled " Nunez the Jew, a Caricatura." But it was not until 1744, when Arthur Pond, the engraver, published a sheaf of about twenty-four caricaturas by Italian artists that the art can be said to have been established here. As it happened, it was one of these that may claim to have been the earliest caricatura done in England of which any record remains. It was engraved by Pond in 1739, from a drawing by Antoine Watteau during his brief visit to England in the winter of 1719-20, being a satirical portrait of Dr. Misaubin, the son of a religious refugee from France, who had established a great, if somewhat questionable reputation in London as the inventor of a famous pill. Watteau represents him not at all unkindly as a tall, handsome figure standing in a graveyard, with the legend " Prenez des Pilules ! " A wider interest attaches itself to this drawing as being the only known work of Watteau in England, and it may be the means of establishing a connection between Watteau and Hogarth and accounting for the extraordinarily fine

2

quality of " The Shrimp Girl "—a masterpiece only discovered in Hogarth's studio after his death, though evidently painted quite early in the century. Mariette, the French connoisseur, wrote on a copy of Pond's print a statement full of inaccuracies as concerning Dr. Misaubin, but there is no reason to doubt that the drawing was made as he says in a London coffee house, and it would hardly have been so if the artist had been alone at the time. Unfortunately, Pond does not say whom the drawing belonged to, or we might discover something very interesting about Watteau's influence on Hogarth. Unfortunately, too, for Dr. Misaubin's reputation, his success was not for the same sort of pills as Holloway's or Beecham's, and he has accordingly been identified with the apothecary in Hogarth's Rake's Progress and also in another print. This, though probably incorrect—for as a matter of fact, Dr. Misaubin was a most reputable and successful practitioner—would strengthen the link between Watteau and Hogarth, both in painting and in caricature.

But it was not Hogarth who carried on the tradition of caricatura. His was a different art, and his remarks on caricatura are set out, from his Analysis of Beauty, at the foot of his etching " The Bench " (Frontispiece). Fielding, too, in his preface to Joseph Andrews in 1742, elaborately distinguishes Hogarth from the caricaturists, and although there were signs here and there of the eventual mingling of other or all kinds of humorous art under a single general term, caricatura continued to enjoy a separate existence for some time to come. As late as 1788, appeared a little book with plates and diagrams entitled " Rules for drawing Caricaturas, with an Essay on Comic Painting." This was by Captain Francis Grose, an antiquary and amateur artist of considerable talent, and his book was in such demand as to be translated both into French and German. By that time caricatura had already been allied with political and social satire, but it still preserved its original characteristic, as the following will usefully show :—

" The art of drawing caricaturas is generally considered as a dangerous acquisition, tending rather to make the possessor feared then esteemed ; but it is certainly an unfair mode of reasoning to urge the abuse to which any art is liable, as an argument against the art itself. To obtain this art the student should begin to draw the human head, from one of those drawing books where the form and proportions constituting beauty, according to the European idea, are laid down . . . . as soon as he has acquired a facility in drawing a head, he may amuse himself in altering the distances of the different lines, marking the places of the features, whereby he will produce a variety of odd faces that will both please and surprize him."

Another of the essential characteristics of caricatura, as distinguished from comical or satirical pictures in general, was independence of publication. This was, perhaps, one of its most prominent features in its infancy, and is still persistent in a very large, varied and interesting class of its descendants whose existence, accordingly, is only discovered by chance, by indiscretion, or by the industrious sifting of the portfolios of artists after their decease, and being thus inherent in the art, it is, or should be, an important influence in the conception of any personal caricature even when, as is now usually the case, it is done expressly for publication. It is the private entrance, so to speak, through which the caricaturist is privileged to approach his subject, and enjoy a few minutes' intimacy that would be denied to the mere journalist or the formal portrait painter. It was, of course, obliterated in the heterogeneous progeny resulting from the union of caricatura with political satire, which was either maliciously or mischievously distorted for party purposes, or simply ignored as unnecessary in merely depicting a conventional figure like Gladstone with his collars or Chamberlain with his monocle. But to the work of Dighton, Ape, Spy and even of Max when he is doing a single portrait, it gives a quality that distinguishes it clearly as caricatura in the true sense of the term.

As for the *inédits* or posthumously published caricatures of artists great and small, these would make a very interesting volume of themselves. To begin with there is Arthur Pond's publication in 1744 of a couple of dozen prints by Ghezzi and earlier Italians, and a larger volume of Ghezzi's published by Oesterreich in 1766. But although these were practically the first of the Italian *caricature* to appear in print, it must be remembered that Ghezzi's popularity was, so to speak, the culmination of the movement in caricatura started by the Carracci over a century earlier, and persisting with considerable activity under the very able efforts of his pupils and followers. Few, if any, of these found their way into print, but there are whole volumes of drawings in the library at Bologna which have never yet been thoroughly explored. Besides Ghezzi's, those in Pond's series, all from drawings in private collections in England include examples by Carlo Maratti, Annibale Carracci, Guercino, Mola and La Fage, all of which induce a desire to see something of the bulk from which these may be taken as samples.

In its origin and early development, then, we see caricatura as a gentle art, at first practised only in the intervals of serious work in the studio of a great school of Italian painters, and in adolescence still only concerned with the harmless amusement of making pleasant fun out of personal absurdities, or perhaps inventing them where none really existed. That such an innocent child should be exploited for more serious purposes, though no doubt inevitable, is much to be regretted for its own sake ; but the results of its employment in political and general satire have been so prodigious that we should rather be thankful for the great gain than deplore the private loss, provided it is not forgotten how great the benefit was that its exploitation conferred.

The credit for this is due to some extent to George, Marquis Townshend, who was perhaps the first and certainly the foremost to devote his very sprightly talent in drawing to personal ridicule of Lord Bute and other Scottish influences in politics soon after the accession of George III in 1760. Walpole mentions his activities in this direction on several occasions in his correspondence, and F. G. Stephens, in compiling the Catalogue of Satirical Prints, praises him very highly for having generally raised the tone of political satire.

Political satire embodied in prints that could be freely circulated, began to be employed in one form or another very soon after the practice of block printing became established, that is to say, in the later years of the fifteenth century. The few very early examples that have survived are probably only a percentage of such essentially perishable material and of ephemeral interest. But with the approach of the Reformation in Europe they came to be employed as the regular ammunition of the contending forces on either side, and their number and importance increased to such an extent that a very considerable body of them is still extant. Towards the end of the seventeenth century they were again resorted to with great intensity in the political and religious struggle between Louis XIV and William of Orange, and though the bulk of them were produced in Holland, both France and England were principally concerned with them, and the establishment of similar production in those two countries was thereby greatly assisted. In France, there was a very strict censorship, but not in England, as the bulky volumes of the British Museum Catalogue of " Satirical Prints " for the earlier part of the eighteenth century very clearly shows.

With the exception of one or two prints by Hubert Gravelot, a French artist who was working in England in the 'forties, there is hardly one of these very humorous and very interesting prints that is of the slightest artistic interest. Romeyn de Hooghe, the Dutchman, was a very capable artist who could fill a large plate with a fine mixture of historical and allegorical rodomontade ; but he was dead before Queen Anne succeeded to the English throne and like her, remained dead; there was no one to succeed him. Rows of gentlemen in flap-tailed coats and enormous wigs, with balloons issuing from their mouths inscribed with political sentiments, were never beautiful, or even funny when associated with some flagrantly vulgar indecency. In two words, political satire was stodgy and inartistic, the one in its conception and the other in its execution, and it was not until the seventeenth century was more than half over that any improvement was perceptible. This improvement was chiefly, if not entirely, due to the employment of caricatura.

There were, doubtless, others besides Townshend who helped to unite caricatura with political satire, and the foundation of the Royal Academy in 1768 brought into practice an immense number of artists whose less serious efforts now found their way into print, and the circulation of " caricatures " became a very active and widely extended business. Early in the 'seventies there were several rivals to the old-established house of Carrington Bowles, print-sellers, notably Humphreys, M. Darly and S. W. Fores—the last mentioned being still extant. Of the artists of better repute who have left caricatures are Cosway, de Loutherbouy, Grimm and Mortimer, and in the 'eighties we first hear of the professional caricaturists, so to speak, headed by Gillray and Rowlandson, with whom were Bunbury, Woodward, Nixon and Isaac Cruikshank. This was the beginning of the florid age of English caricature which, unfortunately, rather dominates its history ; for it soon degenerated into excess, and the flood of production was not always of the purest, especially in its later period under the Regency. If one goes into a print shop, casually asking for caricatures, one is too often shown a portfolio of coloured prints of the very coarsest description, the best of which are Gillray and Rowlandson at their very worst, and the rest fit only for the fire. It has taken Rowlandson's reputation a century to live down this sort of stuff, and he is only now coming to be recognised at his real value for the rest of his extraordinarily brilliant and amusing work. Gillray who has left nothing but his biting satires to judge him by, is still forgotten as an artist, though hardly inferior as a draughtsman to Rowlandson, and more incisive as a caricaturist. Henry William Bunbury and George Moutard Woodward were both of them, like Townshend, amateurs, but unlike him their talents were chiefly employed in social and not in political satire, nor can it be said that in depicting the manners and customs of their own class they showed any decided tendency towards refinement. In general it may be said that the spirit of caricature had escaped from the Italian *fiasco* in which it had been transported to this country, and had permeated the whole atmosphere.

At enim—but someone will say—surely there were political "caricatures" before the reign of George III? Was he indeed the first monarch in Christendom or elsewhere to have his form and features travestied in pen, pencil or paint? Alas! The answer is "Yes"; for how much more attractive, otherwise, would the National Portrait Gallery be. Political satire, it is necessary not only to state, but to insist, was a totally distinct and a totally different art to that of caricatura; it was serious, dull and public, whereas caricatura was flippant, absurd and personal. The alliance between the two has naturally and happily enough resulted in a mutual exchange of these distinct qualities, greatly to their mutual benefit, but it is significant that the modern term " caricature," with all that it includes, is derived from the artistic and not the political side of the union. It is as though a young and charming prince had fallen a prey to some powerful designing and ugly queen, but that in spite of all she brought and acquired for him, he retained his own title and his own personal qualities even when dragged into affairs of state.

Meanwhile, however, though Dr. Johnson ignored the word entirely, the French form of it was gaining ground. In 1771, M. Darly of No. 39 Strand, published " twenty-four caricatures of several Ladies, Gentlemen, Artists, etc." and in 1772 " Volume II of Caricatures, Macarones and Characters by Sundry Ladies, Gentlemen, Artists, etc." Darly was possibly of French extraction, but he was followed as nearly as possible for a cockney by S. W. Fores, progenitor of the present firm in Piccadilly, who published an immense quantity of prints of all sorts which he called " caricatures " or " caracatures " in the 'eighties and 'nineties. In 1790 his prints are " published at his Caracature Warehouse, No. 50 Piccadilly." In 1793 one of them bears an inscription informing us that he " has just fitted up his Exhibition at No. 3 Piccadilly in an entire novel stile," and that " folios of caracatures are lent out." In 1791 a fine print of Catherine of Russia was published by Wm. Holland, No. 50 Oxford Street, with the intimation that " In Holland's Exhibition may be seen the largest collection of caricatures in Europe, admittance, One Shilling." By the end of the century, Mr. Fores had undertaken at least one wholesale transaction, namely, an order from a Mr. Johnes in Wales " for all the caricature prints that had ever been published." This was a taller order than either of the contracting parties had thought, and Fores had to sue Johnes for the price of them, as Johnes had " refused to receive them, on the ground that the collection contained several prints of obscene and immoral subjects ; exclusive of several being duplicates." The judge, it is interesting to note, decided the case very fairly between the two parties. " For prints whose objects are general satire or ridicule of prevailing fashions or manners, I think the plaintiff may recover," he declared, " but I cannot permit him to do so for such whose tendency is immoral or obscene ; nor for such as are libels on individuals and for which the plaintiff might have been rendered criminally answerable for a libel."

There is no doubt that the eighteenth *fin de siècle* threw up an unpleasantly large percentage of prints that were, to say the least of them, extremely vulgar and coarse, but on the other hand we find included in Fores's output of " caricatures " some of Rowlandson's finest and most delicate etchings. Moreover, these prints were ephemeral and never intended for publication in books or periodicals. It was mean of Mr. Johnes to refuse the whole collection, and served him right to have to pay for the bulk of them. The pity is that the judge could not have permanently "impounded the documents," leaving a complete record for historical research workers of " all the caricature prints that had ever been published " at that date.

The birth of modern caricature like that of the Railway System, five years earlier, can be dated with absolute certainty. There are several points of resemblance between the two events. On the 27th September, 1825, George Stephenson, the son of a Northumberland pitman, who had been experimenting with the laying of rails and the manufacture of locomotives—the one dating from the seventeenth century if not far earlier and the other from the opening of the nineteenth—hauled the first train ever put together, loaded with passengers and goods, with an engine he had made himself over a line laid out by himself, and thereby revolutionised the inland transport of the whole world. On the 4th November, 1830, Charles Philipon, the son of a Marseilles manufacturer, who had been experimenting in journalism and lithography—the one dating from the dark ages and the other from the year 1798—produced the first illustrated comic paper, thereby revolutionising the methods of production and distribution of " caricature " in the most extended sense of the term throughout the whole world.

Neither of these two very remarkable men were inventors, but they both of them had both character and genius, and the perceptive faculty of recognising the possibilities of combination which is generally denied to inventors themselves. Trevithick had built and run a locomotive twenty years earlier, and Senefelder had proved lithography as a practical proposition—but neither of them had the genius of Stephenson and Philipon, or the character to tackle and overcome by ceaseless effort the extraordinary difficulties that stood in the way of their final success, and moreover, to carry it continuously further during the whole of their long lives until it had reached a point when it was established universally. . . . An Englishman en route for Port Arthur on the Trans-Siberian line might observe to a Frenchman, with justifiable pride, that they were primarily indebted for this means of transport to George Stephenson ; the Frenchman, pointing to Punch, Simplicissimus, Charivari, Begamot, Travaso, etc., etc., with which they had tried to beguile the intolerable tediousness of the journey, might reply with equal verve " and for these to Charles Philipon."

In calling his first venture " La Caricature " Philipon was really asking for trouble, and as its contents amply justified the title he soon had more of it than perhaps he had reckoned on. After five years of perpetual prosecution the paper was suppressed, though it was soon afterwards revived. But in 1832 he had added a second and still more famous paper to his list, namely, " Charivari," which still flourishes, having been suspended only for a few years during the great war, with something of its old vigour. But these two papers were only a part of an immense output of illustrated matter of all kinds in the nature of caricature, issued by the Maison Aubert, under the management of Philipon, who gathered round him an array of artistic talent which has never been equalled. Among those who are now hardly thought of as being connected with him are Alexandre Decamps, Tony Johannot and Gustave Doré, while of the rest it is only necessary to mention the names of Daumier, Gavarni, Monnier, Traviès and Grandville, to indicate the nature of his activities, while

7

its extent is evidenced by a list of artists who, though of less renown at this particular moment, are never likely to be entirely forgotten. Of all these there is no one who approaches Daumier, who is now being acclaimed as a great painter, so nearly as Doré who was acclaimed one by popular suffrage in the 'seventies, and has consequently vanished from the artistic horizon. It is pathetic to think of the one always wanting to succeed as a painter and never doing so, and the other succeeding in such a way as to efface himself by sheer popularity. But both were geniuses in caricature, and while the one stands supreme, the other is totally forgotten as a caricaturist. But a glance at his lithograph series of Historical Cartoons, or " Different Publics (audiences) à Paris," suffices to show that in spite of the mannered exaggerations and sentimentality of his later work he was entitled to rank both as a draughtsman and a caricaturist pretty nearly equally with Daumier. Even in his earlier book illustrations he shows himself a master both of character and of landscape not entirely inferior to Rowlandson, and with a great deal of his charm, and had he continued as he began to the end of his long career his influence on comic journalism might have saved it from falling quite as low as it did in the 'seventies and 'eighties before its revival with the appearance of " Le Rire." Come forth, Doré, from behind those " great masterpieces," with which you made everyone forget the wonderful achievements of your youth, and let us hear something about you as a caricaturist !

We have an account of Doré's first visit to Paris, when he was only fifteen and a half years old, in his own words (as Blanchard Jerrold records it from Doré's own MS. notes) " In September, 1847, my parents, being called to Paris by serious affairs, took me with them. The idea of returning to the country after seeing this centre of light and learning troubled me much and I thought over the means of remaining. One day I had passed the window of Aubert and Philipon, on the Place de la Bourse, and on returning to the hotel I made some caricatures in the style of those I had seen in the window. While my parents were out I went to the publishers and showed them my sketches. M. Philipon looked kindly and attentively at these beginnings, questioned me as to my position and sent me back to my parents with a letter inviting them to call upon him. They went, and M. Philipon, using all his persuasive eloquence, prevailed upon them to leave me in Paris, telling them that he could at once make use of my talents and pay me for my work." As a matter of fact, Philipon was just starting the third of his most famous periodicals, " Le Journal pour Rire," a specimen issue of which appeared in the following December and the first number on 5th February, 1848. The second had a front page cartoon " Abd-el-Kadir, le Lion du Jour " (as indeed, he was) by Gustave Doré.

For a lad this was not a bad beginning and a little later appeared a volume entitled " Les Travaux d'Hercule, par G. Doré," to which the publishers prefixed a note informing the public that the work had been designed, drawn and lithographed by an artist fifteen years of age, who had taught himself drawing without a master and without classical studies, and that they wished thereby not merely to interest the public in his work, but also to mark his first appearance, as they believed him destined to take distinguished rank in art.

These caricatures of Hercules were a great success and he was kept so busily at work on " Le Journal pour Rire " that he did not produce any more volumes until 1854, when the Crimean War impelled him to his terrific attack

8

on "*La Sainte Russie.*" In 1868 the volume of Historical Cartoons was published by J. C. Hotten in London, which are in a lighter mood again, but the bulk of his work was for the papers and for illustrating books, such as Rabelais' "*Contes Drolatiques*," "*Baron Munchausen*" and his friend Edmond About's "*Le Roi des Montagnes*," in the true spirit of caricature.

One or two of his contributions to the earliest numbers of "*Le Journal*" in 1848 are specially worth noting ; in two instances they anticipate "Punch." "*Exposition pour rire—Salon de* 1848" foreshadowed our "Royal Academy Guyed," and his drawing of Adam and Eve entitled "Peinture primitive—gueux de Serpent, va!" is a gem. A series of subjects in outline, fitted with figures, which includes "Un bal Champêtre dans le Banlieue de Paris," "Salle du bal au Village" and "Un Steeple-chase," must have inspired Richard Doyle in his "Pictures of Society". Jerrold reproduces one of this sort of the interior of the school at Bourg before he left it, which is a miracle of accomplishment.

The amount of caricatures produced by La Maison Aubert during the past twenty years was prodigious. Many of these were reprinted in volumes, and advertisements tell us more or less of their nature. In the fifth number of "*Le Journal pour Rire*" is the following list of "Caricatures, par les principaux dessinateurs du Musée Philipon, du Charivari, du Journal pour Rire, et de la maison Aubert" :—Le Carnaval par Gavarni, Le Carnaval à Paris par le même ; Le nouveau Carnaval, les Coulisses, La Boite aux lettres ; Les Maris Vengés ; Les Artistes ; Les Impressions de Ménage ; Les Lorettes ; Les Enfants Terribles ; Les Beaux jours de la vie (Daumier, 80 sheets) ; Bonnes têtes musicales (Bouchot, 70 sheets) ; Nos Gentilshommes ; Turlupinades ; Souvenirs de Garnison ; A la guerre comme à la guerre ; Les Croquis d'expression (Daumier) ; Militariana (Jacques) ; Moeurs algériennes ; Moeurs britanniques ; L'Amour à Paris (Behr) ; Les Charges parisiennes ; Le Conservatoire de dames ; Ces bons parisiens ; Prophets chariviques ; Les Robert Maquaire par Daumier et Philipon ; Croquis parisiens (E. de Beaumont) ; L'Opéra au 19e siècle ; Au bal de l'Opéra, Les Troupiers français ; Croquis militaires, Les Grisettes (all by Vernier) and Physiognomie des bals publics.

"*Le Musée Philipon*" was advertised in 1848 as in two large quarto volumes and contained over 1,400 plates by Daumier, Eustache, Forest, Gavarni, Grandville, Eugène Lami, Lorentz, Plattier, Trimolet, Vernier and others. In 1850 appeared "Folies caricaturales, deux albums composés chacun de 64 pages toutes remplies de croquades non politiques, par M. M. Bouchot, Cham, Emy, Trimolet," etc. ; and also "Albums de petites caricatures, jolies petites copies par Victor Adam des meilleures caricatures de Carle Vernet :" and "La Revue Comique, Histoire morale politique, philosophique, critique, etc., de l'année 1849, Ornée de 600 dessins, types, caricatures," etc.

But while allowing all the credit to Philipon for the alliance of caricature with journalism, we must take some to ourselves for the development of its modern spirit on this side of the channel. In fact, it is suspiciously probable that he took a leaf or two out of our book. In 1829, the year before the appearance of "La Caricature," Thomas McLean, founder of the still extant Haymarket firm, had published "Metamorphoses du Jour, or Frivolities of the day," by Grandville—some thirty or so of the seventy-one numbered plates published in Paris, with English translations (but evidently by a

9

Frenchman) of the legends attached to them. In the same year he began publishing the famous series of political satires in lithograph by John Doyle, over the mysterious signature " H.B.," which continued for over ten years and ran to nearly a thousand. This looks as though he had either been first in realising the practical possibilities of lithography, or had been in touch with Philipon ; and in 1830 he started his regular issue of " McLean's Caricature Sheets," also in lithograph, which ran very successfully for six years.

Nobody just at the present moment cares twopence about anything of this date—it is, so to speak, dead out of focus. Any schoolboy could tell you more about William the Conqueror than about William the Fourth, and perhaps rightly enough. But the Reform Bill was only one symptom of the changes that were maturing in this short reign, and the burning of the Houses of Parliament, without the intervention or invention of a Guy Fawkes, another. For our present purpose it may suffice to say that with the death of Rowlandson in 1828, there was room for a successor who could do something to shape the tendencies of the next generation and eclipse the florid absurdities of the elder Cruikshank, Heath and a host more. John Doyle was certainly the man who filled the bill, for George Cruikshank instead of following in father's footsteps, took a higher and broader road, and became in another age another Hogarth. If Doyle's subjects had not been so purely political, they would have a better chance with the collectors against the pretty sentimentalities of Wheatley, Bigg and even Morland ; for they are beautifully drawn, and when coloured as many of them were in delightful tones, they are quite as charming and much more amusing—for they are first and foremost personal caricatures.

Another famous caricaturist of this reign was Robert Seymour, who was less, much less, of an artist, but like Doré, really demands to be remembered. " The publisher of his collected edition of Seymour's humorous sketches," writes Hotten in the 'sixties, " conceived that the present generation might find some amusement in another issue of the droll pictures and comicalities which set the world laughing thirty years since. Although our tastes have considerably altered since those days of shaved chins, black satin stocks, high shirt collars and, as our mammas will remember, leg-of-mutton sleeves, sandals and projecting bonnets of the cottage shape—this, the *very latest* fashion—our appreciation of genuine fun is quite as vigorous, requiring, indeed, much less of violent contrast, and far less exaggeration of style than formerly. The little troubles, the smaller eventualities, the nicer differences of life appear to be a sufficient food for present merry-making. If we demand prussic acid and nine-inch stilettos in our modern novels, an unclaimed *chignon*, a five-haired moustache, or an unstable " calf " which has twisted to the front of John Thomas's leg, is material sufficient and inexhaustible for our weekly supply of laughter. It was John Leech more than any other artist, who assisted the milder taste in our national fun. The finer shades of humour rather than the old broad form of wit appear to characterise the popular taste of the present day."

Seymour's career, so unhappily ended before he was forty, is very interesting as showing the state of things in the world of caricature from the inside. As a boy, Severn told him that if he (Severn) saw an old woman fall down in the street, the artist so far predominated in him that instead of helping her to rise, it was his custom to take out his sketch book and make a picture of her. This must have been very bad for Seymour, because he was at that age trying to take art very seriously indeed, purchasing plaster casts of different parts of the body for study ; and his first exhibited painting, at the Royal Academy, was thus described in the catalogue : " The Christians deterred by the terrors of enchantment from felling timber to construct their machines of annoyance." But his appreciation of the comic and humorous increased with years, although his friend and patron, Sir Richard Phillips, the publisher of " A Million of Facts," persisted in prophesying that he would one day become President of the Royal Academy. Among his earliest efforts were two whimsical etchings published by Creed, entitled " A Musical Genius " and " A Man of Taste and Feeling," which he happened to show to McLean, who was the nearest approach in England to Philipon across the channel, and he was so pleased with them as to take them at the artist's own price with a promise to take anything else in the same vein. To these and similar caricatures, Seymour affixed the name of *Shortshanks*, but George Cruikshank resented this playful liberty taken with his name, and it was at once dispensed with. Another of his early successes was " Unexpected Arrival by Steam," a stout lady sent through a drawing-room window plump into the midst of a fashionable tea-party by the accidental explosion of her locomotive. Of his political caricatures may be mentioned one of George IV and Lord Eldon weeping over a dead giraffe, and an elaborate satire on the then existing system of taxation, entitled " Heaven and Earth," the lower half of which showed a population starving and without employment, while the smoke from the steam factories around rolls up in clouds full of money to form a firmament on which the great officers in Church and State enjoyed the good things of this life.

In 1830, Seymour was engaged by McLean to illustrate a series of political and social caricatures to be entitled " The Looking Glass," which in his hands became an admirable medium of satire. The portraits of the leading characters were here cleverly introduced, among others an excellent one of the celebrated Edward Irving, sitting in his chapel, and awaiting the inspiration of the Unknown Tongue. It continued monthly till his death in 1836. " The Omnibus " was another series, etched on copper, and " The Heiress," which was a pictorial novel in six plates, each plate consisting of four or five subjects representing " the concatenation of incidents and events which conduct a young woman from a state of dependence to a Gretna Green alliance with a gallant captain."

Seymour soon became acquainted with Gilbert Abbot A'Beckett, well known by his connection with " Punch " and other facetious periodicals, who was bringing out one called "Figaro in London," and as Seymour's name was very popular the editor was glad to secure his services for the illustrations, which were very successful. One of his letters to Seymour lets us into the secret of their composition : "Dear Sir, I am sorry I cannot see you ; I am considerably puzzled for subjects, though the caricature must certainly be on the collision between the two Houses of Parliament. Could you invent something funny on this point ? Or could anything humorous be made of John Bull standing between the Tory Peers on the one side and the Whig Commons on the other, headed by the King, each holding by and tugging against one another to get his coat from his back ? Or could you make something of Grey emptying a bucket of Whig nobility into the House, which swamps the Tories and carries away the Bishops, taking them all off their legs and hurrying them away in all directions ? I can think of nothing better myself. Please send me a sketch as soon as possible on Monday."

Owing to a quarrel with A'Beckett, Seymour withdrew from the "Figaro," but resumed after a couple of years when Henry Mayhew was appointed editor, and his reappearance was conspicuously advertised on the front page. Another editorial letter, this time from Mayhew, is interesting also : " Will you be so kind as to proceed with the design I gave you, which to prevent accident I shall here repeat ? Represent the Queen (Adelaide) as a German Frow, as Cobbett calls her, making her Coronet resemble those small caps the drovers wear, playing the hurdy-gurdy and leading the King, who is to represent a monkey, about with a string, and a very capital one I think he will make. Make him looking up in the Queen's face as if afraid of her. You can form, I think, the head of the hurdy-gurdy into Wellington's face. You, perhaps, recollect there is generally a sort of scroll at the end of these instruments which I think admirably suited for that purpose. . . ."

But if Seymour's reputation was not strong enough to survive his generation and has been overshadowed by those of Doyle, Leech and Cruikshank, it is all the more due to him to mention that almost his last undertaking became, in other hands, an imperishable monument of humour. The year before his death (by his own hand) he had been disappointed with the effect of his gardening operations, for he was very fond of horticultural pursuits and took great pains in cultivating a very nice garden which was attached to his house. It was suggested to him that the misfortunes of an amateur gardener might be made the subject of some humorous drawings, and after revolving the idea in his mind for a short time, he resolved upon converting it into something of a sporting character, and said it should be " Pickwick and his Club." After a considerable amount of modification of his original idea, it was arranged that Dickens should write the letterpress, and the first number appeared appropriately enough on 1st April, 1836.

Both in England and France, the success of Philipon's periodicals soon resulted in a further extension of the domain of caricature which can hardly, as before, be suggested in terms of a matrimonial alliance. The two partners, Caricatura and Satirical Print may, on this occasion, be said to have amalgamated with the old-established business of Journalism—or perhaps, at any rate, entered into a permanent arrangement with it for the handling and distribution of all but a very small part of their products. Again, the advantages being mutual, the results were prodigious, and they have subsisted with ever increasing volume until to-day there is hardly a newspaper or periodical in which caricature, in one form or another, is not a sensible contribution to its success. The broadside, the caricature sheet, the comic print, are all things of the past—even the valentine survives only in the vulgar post-card still to be seen in the shop-windows in back streets. Henceforth, caricature was to be regularly housed, clothed and fed by journalism, and its production and circulation continued to increase steadily until to-day it is practically unlimited.

For the first few years this was confined to France. But in 1841 England decided that there was something in it, and paid Philipon the compliment of adopting his title for the first and still foremost English comic paper, " Punch or the London Charivari." But how many of its thousands of readers, it might be asked, could tell you what a " Charivari " is, why " Punch " was called the " London Charivari," or have ever heard of Charles Philipon ?

Germany was the next country to follow the lead ; in 1845, " *Fliegende Blätter* " made its first appearance in Munich, and in 1848, " *Kladderadatsch* " in Berlin : so that there are now four of the leading comic papers in Europe well on their way to centenarianism and without any of the more conspicuous signs of dotage. In Italy, Turin took the lead with " *Il Fischietto* " in 1848 and not long afterwards " *Papagallo* " in Bologna became still more famous. In Vienna there were sooner or later, " *Kikeriki* " and " *Figaro*," in Zurich, " *Nebelspalter*," in St. Petersburg, " *Strekoza*," in Lisbon, " *Os Puntos nos ii* " (the dots on the i's), in Brussels, " *Eulenspiegel*," in Cracow, " *Djabel*." These are just one or two of the more important in the mid-nineteenth century, but there were scores of others which, though now forgotten, will most likely prove to be very valuable aids to the historian of their period in time to come. The first indication of this probability may be seen in a little book compiled by J. Grand-Carteret, after the retirement of Bismarck in 1890, in which he has collected over a hundred cartoons from the European papers concerning the great Chancellor's activities during the previous quarter of a century. But this deals only with politics, indeed, with only a particular section of that, and is a mere sample of what was accomplished by the " caricature " press at this date. For to bring the various branches of caricature thus together permanently under one roof was certain to influence their growth and to blend them in varying fashion according to circumstances as had never been done before. The three partners, Personal, Political and Social, were more or less active on different occasions and at different dates, but broadly speaking, the result has been that Personal, while still giving his title of " caricature " to the whole concern, has been relegated to a minor share, Political has been given the best suite of rooms to himself, and Social has usurped the rest of the premises, which he has used in such a way as to attract a good deal more custom than the other two would ever have attracted without him ; such at any rate, was the position in " Punch " during the later Victorian period, and is still. Tenniel's dignified cartoons and Sambourne's allegorical compositions are quite apart from the social effusions of Du Maurier and Keene, but all of them are, if one may say so, under the same hat, inspired by the same spirit which, however different from the Italian original, is in fact, the spirit of caricature. If we miss the absurd portraits of actual people, which in the French papers were the most formidable feature, we have Leech's " Mr. Briggs," Keene's " 'Arry " and Du Maurier's " Postlethwaite," etc., which are comparable with Daumier's " Robert Macaire," Monnier's " Monsieur Prudhomme " and Traviès' " Mayeux."

One very notable thing resulting from the admission of Journalism into the partnership is that there is no hard and fast line left between what is really caricature and what is simply an illustration of a " funny joke." It may be objected that there never was more than an imaginary line, and that it was never either hard or fast. But this is scarcely true. Rowlandson's subjects for example, as may be seen in Plates 4 and 5, require no explanation beyond their mere title to raise a laugh. They characterise, in caricature, the Punchbowl Club and The Visit to the Picture Gallery. As an extreme instance on the other side may be mentioned a spirited sketch in a recent number of a Madrid paper " *Gutierriez*," where a man and his wife are gazing at a poster of a prancing hippopotamus. There is nothing very laughable in

13

that, but when we hear the man saying " By the bye (aproposito), have you written to your mother ? " it assumes an intensely comic character.   Then, in fact, we realise that the artist has illustrated the joke exceedingly well, and has enabled us to enjoy it as the mere narration of it could never have done. It does not require a parenthetical " (*Catching sight of Hippopotamus*) " to explain it.   About half-way between these extremes is a picture of Leech's of two elderly men fishing from a punt, the one observing to the other " What I enjoy about fishing is not so much the sport, but the delicious repose "—while only a couple of yards behind them is the prow of a boat blindly urged at top speed by two young Cockneys straight for the punt.   Max's cartoon of " Rossetti in his back garden at Chelsea "—the very place in which these words are now falling from my pen—is another which is even farther from the line than Rowlandson's, for it is essentially Italian *caricatura*, depending for its effect solely on the absurdly distorted portraits of the distinguished personages gathered there, every one of whom is easily recognisable at a glance, and rendered ten times more absurd and more recognisable by their respective expressions and attitudes.   Here is the caricaturist *in excelsis*.   There is not a line in the whole composition, except the brick wall, which is within measurable distance of actuality, but it might well be filed for reference at the National Portrait Gallery as a certain test of the identity of any disputed portrait of any of the group.

The revival of purely personal caricature in this country, or rather the assertion of its claim to a separate existence independent of humorous or satirical circumstances, dates from the foundation of Vanity Fair in 1869. By a great stroke of luck there were two artists then in England, one Italian and the other French, in whose hands the success of the venture was assured. Carlo Pellegrini, better known by his signature as " Ape," and J. J. Tissot, whose signatures varied.   Not until later was the latter superseded by Leslie Ward, " Spy," and many of the finest portraits in the early numbers are Tissot's.   Save for a series of European sovereigns, all of which were represented with some politically significant symbolism, these portraits were essentially characteristic, and as he had some very distinguished material to work upon their interest is no less than their excellence, which consists chiefly in their beautiful handling as light, good-humoured and hardly exaggerated pictures of the men as he saw and knew them.   Darwin, Froude, Tait, Matthew Arnold, to take a few of the most notable, are all a little " ridiculous " in the emphasis given to personal traits, but it is not to make fun of them, but rather to bring out the human qualities that so persistently elude the academician in a solemn portrait.   There they are, standing, sitting or leaning, in a greater variety according to their several dispositions than may be found in the whole long gallery of Ape's or Spy's that came after them or Richard Dighton's before them.   Perhaps it is hardly fair to acquit Tissot of becoming monotonous in so small a series, but both Ape and Spy certainly fell into monotony, and even in their first flights were never quite so charmingly penetrating as Tissot, who seemed to mix the actual and the absurd with such exactly-rightness, that one feels one could recognise these people at a glance from his portraits if they ever reappeared on earth as they were.

In Another World, as the western mind conceives it, we should be much more likely to recognise personages (those we have never seen) from their caricatures than from an Academy portrait, or photograph.   For that and not mere exaggeration or comicality is the real test of a successful caricature. It is the character of the person with something intensive added, which may or may not be funny or pleasing, but which certainly expresses the spirit in which it is executed.

For this reason alone the artistic side of the subject is worth considering apart from its general history; for this is just where art, of its own motion and subject to no academical constriction, most naturally shows itself as of a different order from the common ranks of skill and accomplishment, and when we extend our view from personal caricature to that of subjects, political, religious or social, we shall find that while this principle is equally applicable, it is, in addition, a very safe guide in enabling us to take a general view of the whole subject by the selection of such examples as are conspicuous rather for their excellence as artistic designs than for any mere absurdity or ridiculosity.

With the work of the seventeenth, eighteenth and nineteenth centuries, time has shown such a generalisation to be fairly true. With the exception of Townshend, Bunbury, Woodward and Seymour, all of whom were amateurs, all the artists named in the preceding pages were men of high accomplishment and almost all well known for other work than caricature. When we come to the twentieth century it is a little more difficult to discriminate, in the enormous quantity of newspaper production, between what is likely to survive its occasion and be handed down for the delight or benefit of posterity, and what is merely cute, funny and apt for the journalistic moment. But is it necessary to do so? Vine leaves in the hair are not the same thing as laurels on the brow. And is it desirable? Discrimination is an exercise of the mind which is a little out of step with the present state of things. The war has shaken everyone into ridges, like grains of sand on a piano when somebody thumps, and the motoring, sports, science, gaspers and other lines cut across the old divisions or connections between all sorts and conditions of men and nothing is the same as it was twenty years ago—not even for the caricaturist. This is in many ways a distinct gain for him, but there are also losses.

Any society that is not freely recruited from the comparatively lower classes rapidly tends to fossilisation. In these days this tendency is seldom allowed a chance of becoming dangerous, but it is not so long since it gave the caricaturist a very fair share of his opportunities. Some of the earlier cartoons in "Vanity Fair" were much truer to the life and habit of the man than might be believed by the younger generation to-day. The wives of the Victorian clergy, secure in their blameless and busy lives from the pencil of fun, have, nevertheless, enriched the albums of their younger relations with carte de visite photographs of themselves which Time is slowly but surely maturing into collector's gems. In those days, it was often said, by way of a mild joke, that society was getting very mixed, but now that the process is complete and still continuing, nobody thinks it worth saying. This, again, is a loss to the caricaturist, but one for which he is compensated by the total absence of any bounds or limits whatever. The market is now open, and the various occupants of the old pens wander and intermingle freely in social space. The peer turns journalist and the journalist peer, the bishop scientist and the scientist preacher. The chauffeur disdains the vernacular of the cabman, which is taken up by the admiral or the country parson. The brewer has ceased to be a personality, having long since been dissolved, if not liquidated, as a limited company.   The country mansion is now an asylum, of one sort or another, and the town one a suite of offices or residential flats.   The horse, the top hat and the petticoat have all of them had their day, and the skirt, it is probable, is almost on its last legs.   Ladies and gentlemen are merely words used to open public speeches or to indicate public conveniences.   Hyde Park is only resorted to (before sunset) by the frumps.   Dress and deportment are alike free of the old traditions and a strain is thus thrown on the caricaturist in composing the " ritratto ridicolo di cui siansi esagerati i defetti," which but for the example of Picasso and the doctrine of " significant form," might have proved altogether too great for him.   The consequence is that all bounds have been loosened, and angles and bulges have resulted which transcend the marvels of the face-lifting treatment, and we are back again at the very starting point of true caricature.

RANDALL DAVIES

Presumed portraits of the engraver Thomassin and
wife ; Callot's revenge following his dismissal from
the engraver's studio
*From a pen-and-wash drawing in the possession of
Monsieur Paul Prouté, reproduced in Sieure's " Vie
Artistique de Callot "*

LEONARDO DA VINCI

DRAWING OF GROTESQUE HEADS
Venice Academy

PLATE 2   AN EIGHTEENTH CENTURY ARTIST

London Published by G. Humphrey 27 S.t James's S.t May 14 1821

A Pas de Deux or Love at first Sight.

How I'd love you all the day | If with me you'd fondly stray
Every Night we'd Kiss and Play | Over the Hills and far away.

From " *The Attorney General's Charges against the Late Queen.   Brought forward in
the House of Peers, on Saturday, August* 19, 1820.   *Illustrated with Fifty Coloured
Engravings* "   (*London :   Published by G. Humphrey,* 27, *St. James's Street*)

"LE CAPITAINE FRACASSE"

From " The History of French Etching " by Dr. Leipnik
(John Lane, The Bodley Head, Limited)

PLATE 4

THOMAS ROWLANDSON

"THE PUNCH BOWL"

By courtesy of Randall Davies, Esq.

PLATE 5

THOMAS ROWLANDSON

"THE ACADEMY"

By courtesy of Thomas Girtin, Esq.

" Omnium Gatherum No. 1 "

" Old Ways and New Ways No. 1 "

MODES AND MANNERS OF THE EARLY 19th CENTURY

From " Caricature Scrap Book "

PLATE 7

HONORÉ DAUMIER

"DEUX AVOCATS" (TWO BARRISTERS)   *Ionides Collection, Victoria and Albert Museum*

PLATE 8

"HOTEI"

From Hokusai's " Shashin Gwafu"

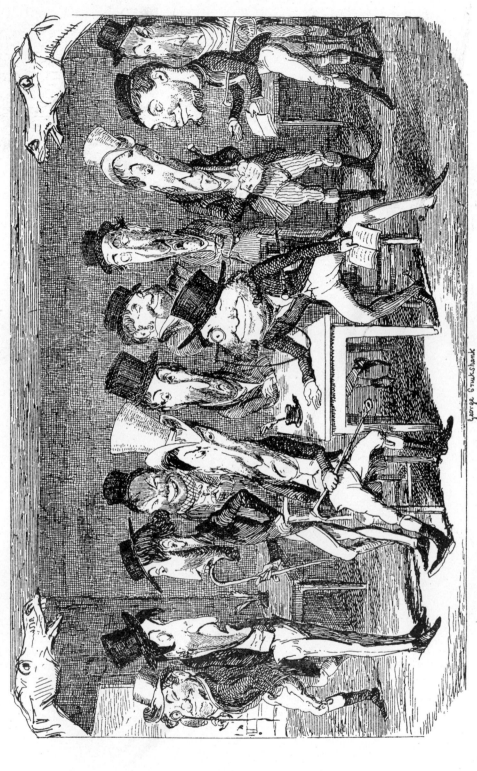

George Cruikshank

MAY — Settling for the Derby – Long odds and long faces

From " The Comic Almanack " (First Series, 1835-1843)

By courtesy of Chatto and Windus

PLATE 10   RICHARD DOYLE

MANNERS · AND · CVSTOMS · OF · Yᴱ · ENGLYSHE · IN · 1849 ·   No 3.

Yᴱ FASHONABLE · WORLDE · TAKYNGE · ITS · EXERCYSE · IN · HYDE · PARKE ·

PLATE 11

Reproduced by courtesy of H. Nöldecke, Hattorf am Harz, Germany

PLATE 12   EDWARD LEAR

There was an Old Man on a hill, who seldom, if ever, stood still;
He ran up and down in his grandmother's gown,
Which adorned that Old Man on a hill.

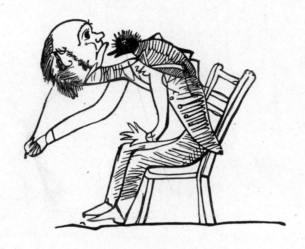

There was an Old Man of Quebec,—a beetle ran over his neck;
But he cried, "With a needle I'll slay you, O beadle!"
That angry Old Man of Quebec.

From " The Book of Nonsense " by Edward Lear (Frederick Warne and Co.)

"THE PERILS OF PIANO PLAYING" (enlarged from the original illustration)

Reproduced by permission of the Proprietors of "Punch"

FROM " ALLY SLOPER'S CHRISTMAS HOLIDAYS " 1881-85

By courtesy of Gilbert Dalziel, Esq.

PLATE 15   PHIL MAY

SO LIKELY!
SCENE—*Bar of a Railway Refreshment Room*
Barmaid: " Tea, Sir ? "   Mr. Boozy: " Tea ! ! ! Me ! ! ! ! "

(*Reproduced by permission of the Proprietors of " Punch "*)

"WHITECHAPEL: SATURDAY MORNING"

By courtesy of M. H. Spielmann, Esq.

" Voila un triste Salon . . . c'ést dégoûtant . . . Vous n'avez rien
ici vous ? " " Bon Dieu, non ! Et vous ? " " Ni moi non plus "

PLATE 18   SPY

MEN OF THE DAY, NO. 33. (CHARLES DARWIN)

"Natural Selection"

From " Vanity Fair "

MEN OF THE DAY, NO. 38. (JAMES ANTHONY FROUDE)

" He created Henry VIII, exploded Mary Stuart, and
demolished Elizabeth "

From " Vanity Fair "

PLATE 20   HENRI DE TOULOUSE-LAUTREC

YVETTE GUILBERT
Linger-longer-loo
By courtesy of the Editor of " Le Rire "

*Déplorable dépérissement occasioné par une forte fièvre politique
compliquée d'avertissements*

"LA LEVRETTE DE MADAME LA DUCHESSE"

From " Nos Humoristes"

PLATE 23   CARAN D'ACHE

(Revue Illustrée.)

" Comment Polyte se représente un bal dans le Grand Monde "

From " Nos Humoristes "

"ANIMAL SPIRITS"

No. XII.—Outside Exeter Hall

(*Reproduced by permission of the Proprietors of " Punch "*)

PLATE 25   HERMANN PAUL

"LA BELLE OTERO"
From "Nos Humoristes"

"REUNION ELECTORALE"

From " Nos Humoristes " by Adolphe Brisson (Librairie Georges Baranger, Paris)

"'SHADOWING' MEMBERS OF PARLIAMENT"
(*Reproduced by permission of the Proprietors of "Punch"*)

PLATE 28

CHARLES LÉANDRE

M. E. DRUMONT

From " Nos Humoristes "

M. CLÉMENCEAU
From " Nos Humoristes "

SCENES FROM GERMAN CLERICAL LIFE

" Sage mir, Gotthold, ist unsere irdische Liebe nicht doch Sündhaft ? " —
" O nein, Mathilde, sünhaft ist nur das Vergnügen "

By courtesy of the Editor of " Simplicissimus "

"THE UNKNOWN GOD"

By courtesy of Geoffrey T. Blackwell, Esq.

PLATE 32

H. M. BATEMAN

Mr. DERWENT WOOD

By courtesy of The Chelsea Arts Club

PLATE 33

H. M. BATEMAN

Mr. CECIL KING

By courtesy of The Chelsea Arts Club

SPRINGTIME PURSUITS

From Volume 1 *of Kyōsai's* "*Sui-Gwa*" (*Drunken Sketches*)

SELF PORTRAIT, "BOY ON A RUSTIC SEAT"

PLATE 36   BRUNO PAUL

WARUM?

"Was hat nun eigentlich die preussische Regierung mit dem Ankauf
der 'Hibernia' bezweckt?" — "Na, wollte sich zur Abwechslung
auch mal unter der Erde blamieren"

By courtesy of the Editor of "Simplicissimus"

"ENGLISH CIVILISATION"

By courtesy of the Editor of "Simplicissimus"

"THE ROYAL ACADEMY OPENS"

Art holding the Mirror up to Nature, Burlington House, 1913

From "Cartoons: Will Dyson" (Daily Herald)

PLATE 39   RUDOLF WILKE

BEFORE THE SISTINE MADONNA OF RAPHAEL

I.

— — Das ist göttliche Kunst — —

By courtesy of the Editor of " Simplicissimus "

BEFORE THE SISTINE MADONNA OF RAPHAEL
II.
Sakrament ! — Sakrament !

By courtesy of the Editor of " Simplicissimus "

II

I

III

HÖHERE LAKAIEN

"Was sagen Sie denn zu der neuesten Uniformverordnung,
Herr Kollege?"

"Hm — — —."

"Uebrigens möchte ich da nichts gesagt haben. Im gegenteil,
man kann nicht genug betonen dass die Verordnung doch ganz
entschieden wesentliche Verbesserungen enthäit."

By courtesy of the Editor of "Simplicissimus"

DRAWING FOR LITTLE MORITZ'S SCRIBBLING BOOK

"Wie sich der Moritz die 'Löwen des Salons' vorstellt"

By courtesy of the Editor of "Fliegende Blätter"

PLATE 43 OLAF GULBRANSSON

GEORG BRANDES
By courtesy of the Editor of " Simplicissimus "

GABRIELE D'ANNUNZIO

By courtesy of the Editor of " Simplicissimus "

PLATE 45   POY

"GOVERNMENT GUS"

"DILLY AND DALLY"

By courtesy of the Editor of " The Evening News "

PLATE 46

SEM

"Tout de même, il a le chic Anglais !"

MAURICE DE ROTHSCHILD   JAMES DE ROTHSCHILD

PLATE 47

DORIS ZINKEISEN

JAZZ BAND

PLATE 48

E. THÖNY

GUILDHALL BANQUET

" Wir Diplomaten würden uns glänzend vertragen, wenn nur die Weltgeschichte
nicht wäre "

By courtesy of the Editor of " Simplicissimus "

MARX—DER CHARAKTER

"Und schreiben Sie, bitte, in mein Abgangszeugnis, dass ich im Lauf der
Jahre allen Richtungen treu gedient habe"

By courtesy of the Editor of "Simplicissimus"

PLATE 50   TELL

GROCK

ISRAEL ZANGWILL

PLATE 52   RYSZARD ANDERSEN

STRESEMANN
By courtesy of the Editor of " Muchy " (Warsaw)

HARRY TATE

PLATE 54   W. HEATH ROBINSON

"THE EARLY QUEUERS"

Mrs. Broadgusset to Mr. B. (an inveterate first-nighter)

"It's not that I mind waiting until the theatre's ready, but suppose they change their
mind and turn it into a town hall"

By courtesy of the Editor of " The Bystander "

METROPOLITAN POLICE

SARAH BERNHARDT

From " Carcasses Divines " (Societé du Mercure de France)

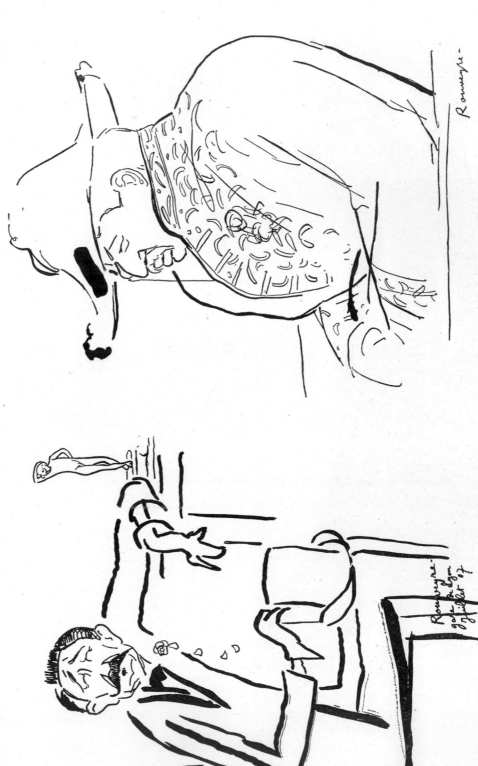

PLATE 57

ANDRÉ ROUVEYRE

PAUL BOURGET

COMTE ROBERT DE MONTESQUIOU

From " Carcasses Divines " (Société du Mercure de France)

PLATE 58

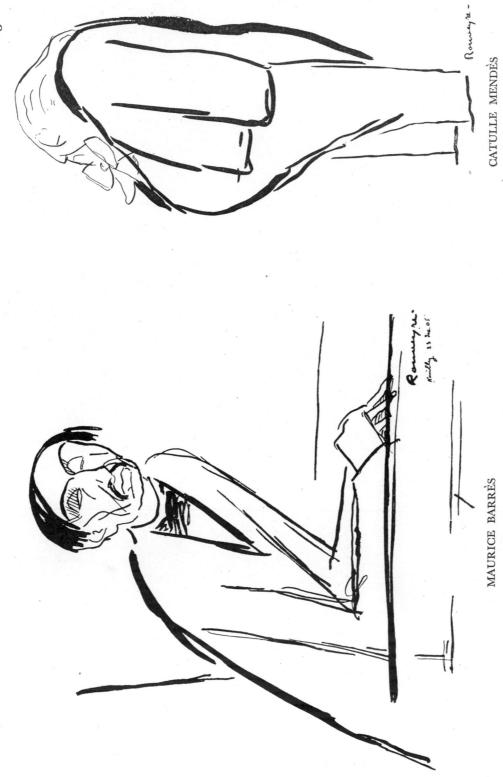

ANDRÉ ROUVEYRE

CATULLE MENDÈS

MAURICE BARRÈS
From " Carcasses Divines " (Société du Mercure de France)

PLATE 59

CÉCILE SOREL

ANATOLE FRANCE

From " Carcasses Divines "
(Société du Mercure de France)

LORD HALDANE AS LORD CHANCELLOR
By courtesy of Vernon Roberts, Esq.

PLATE 61   KAPP

THE HON. Mr. JUSTICE AVORY
By courtesy of Curt Dehn, Esq.

SIR ERNEST POLLOCK, MASTER OF THE ROLLS
By courtesy of Curt Dehn, Esq.

PLATE 63   EDMUND DULAC

LÉON BAKST

GEORGE BERNARD SHAW

GEORGE MOORE

PLATE 66   ARTHUR WATTS

"CHANSON TRISTE"

Reproduced by permission of the Proprietors of "Punch"

"STUDY OF A DETECTIVE MINGLING WITH THE CROWD AT A NIGHT CLUB"

Reproduced by permission of the Proprietors of "Punch"

PLATE 68   CECIL BEATON

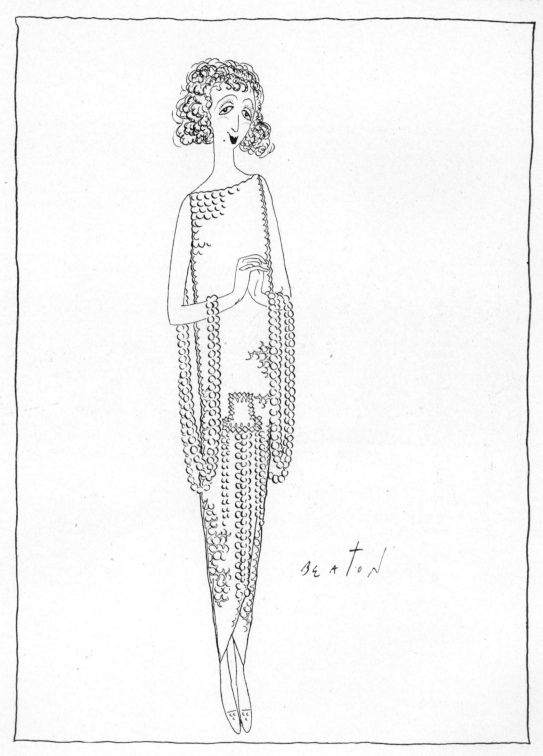

BINNIE HALE IN "PUPPETS" AT THE VAUDEVILLE

THE LADY DIANA COOPER

"MUSSOLINI AND THE STORK"

By courtesy of the Editor of "Kladderadatsch"

PLATE 71

WERNER HAHMANN

RÉPUBLIQUE FRANÇAISE AND MONSIEUR POINCARÉ

By courtesy of the Editor of " Kladderadatsch "

PLATE 72

FISH

Mr. TEDDY BROWN OF THE CAFÈ DE PARIS

By courtesy of the Editor of " Eve "

FISH

ANITA LOOS

By courtesy of the Editor of " Eve "

WILLY CLARKSON

By courtesy of the Editor of " London Calling "

"H'M! PLEASE CLOSE THE GATE ON YOUR WAY OUT!"

By courtesy of the Editor of " The Saturday Evening Post "

PLATE 76   PEARL BINDER

"WIFE OF AN IMPORTANT PERSON"

ARNOLD BENNETT AND EDWARD KNOBLOCK

PLATE 78   MAX BEERBOHM

Mr. OSBERT AND Mr. SACHEVERELL SITWELL

From " Observations " by Max Beerbohm (William Heinemann Ltd.)

"HENRI MURGER"

From " Synthèses Littéraires et extra Littéraires " (Editions Mornay, Paris)

SYDNEY WEBB

By courtesy of the Editor of " The New Leader "

PLATE 81   LOW

A STRANGER ASKS THE ORACLES THE WAY TO CIVILIZATION.

By courtesy of the Editor of " The Evening Standard "

THE CONSERVATOCIALISTS.

MR. AUSTEN MAXTON.   MR. J RAMSAY BALDWIN.   MR. WINSTON KIRKWOOD.   SIR W. JOYNSON-LANSBURY

(Dedicated to that section of the Tory party who, whenever the Government shows signs of life, accuse it of Socialism.)

UNCLE THOMAS'S CABINET.

By courtesy of the Editor of " The Evening Standard "

ANNUAL INQUEST ON THE BRITISH THEATRE.

By courtesy of the Editor of " The Evening Standard "

"AN OLD FAVOURITE"

HILAIRE BELLOC
By courtesy of the Editor of " The New Statesman "

PLATE 86　　　　　　　　　　　　　　　　　ABEL FAIVRE

"— Monsieur le Ministre, excusez　.　.　.　on ferme ! "

By courtesy of the Editor of " Le Rire "

"DAS ENFANT TERRIBLE"

By courtesy of the Editor of " Kladderadatsch "

PLATE 88   EDWARD BAWDEN

"MARIONETTES"

Miss Salaman   Basil Taylor   Lucy Norton   Billy

LORD ROBERT CECIL

PLATE 90   WILLIAM AUERBACH-LEVY

EUGENE O'NEILL

(Cut and printed on wood by Harry de Maines)

JED HARRIS
(*Cut and printed on wood by Harry de Maines*)

PLATE 92   SAVA

SIR ARTHUR CONAN DOYLE

THE RT. HON. SIR AUSTEN CHAMBERLAIN, M.P.

SOME RADIO IMPROVEMENTS

NO. I. SECOND CHILDHOOD'S HOUR

"Will Willum Wetwhistle of Wimbledon look under the bath chair in Grandad's room"

PLATE 95   MATT

"POINCARÉ"

"THE PREMIER"

PLATE 97   NERMAN

DELYSIA
By courtesy of the Editor of " The Tatler "

JOSÉ COLLINS AND KINGSLEY LARK IN "THE LAST WALTZ"

By courtesy of the Editor of "The Tatler"

PLATE 99   ENRIQUE ECHEA

"ARTE DRAMATICO"

"COCIDO A LA ESPANÒLA"
By courtesy of the Editor of "La Esfera" (Madrid)

"MUSICA, ARTE, CAFE Y LITERATURA"
By courtesy of the Editor of " La Esfera" (Madrid)

PLATE 101

OSCAR BERGER

ANNA PAVLOVA

VALESKA GERZ

CANADIAN CELEBRITIES

H. E. The Rt. Hon. The Viscount Willingdon, G.C.S.I., G.C.M.G., G.C.I.E., G.B.E.

By courtesy of the Editor of " The Canadian Forum "

PLATE 104   AUBREY HAMMOND

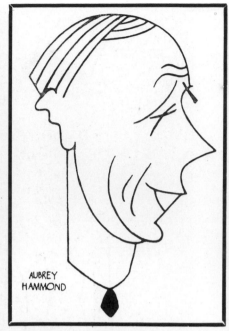

JOE ZELLI   FITZ, OF CIRO'S AT DEAUVILLE

By courtesy of Messrs. Hiram Walker and Sons, Ltd.

PHILIP GUEDALLA   MICHAEL SADLEIR

By courtesy of Messrs. Constable and Company, Ltd.

PROFESSOR HENRY TONKS

From " Eighty-eight Cartoons by Powys Evans" (*The Cayme Press*)

PLATE 106   POWYS EVANS

COLONEL GEORGE HARVEY, SOMETIME AMERICAN AMBASSADOR TO THE
COURT OF ST. JAMES'

From " Eighty-eight Cartoons by Powys Evans " (*The Cayme Press*)

SIR CHARLES HOLMES

From " Eighty-eight Cartoons by Powys Evans " (*The Cayme Press*)

PLATE 108   POWYS EVANS

SIR HENRY CURTIS BENNETT

From " Eighty-eight Cartoons by Powys Evans " (The Cayme Press)

BEFORE THE FOOTLIGHTS OF ÆSTHETICISM

QUIZ

Mr ROGER FRY

From " Eighty-Eight Cartoons by Powys Evans " (The Cayme Press)

Mr. RAMSAY MACDONALD AND THE RAGAMUFFIN
By courtesy of Messrs. Rowntree and Company, Ltd.

PLATE III   SAMA

—Está usted grave.   Se va usted a morir. . . . .es que trabaja mucho ?
—Sí, doctor.   Me paso el día trabajando en la Bolsa. . . . .
—Pues deje usted de ir por allí si no quiere morirse.   Ya sabe usted :
la Bolsa, o la vida. . . . .

By courtesy of the Editor of " Buen Humor " (Madrid)

КТО КОГО БОИТСЯ ("I CARE FOR NOBODY")

БЮРОКРАТ:—Говорят, что я боюсь критики! Чепуха! Посмотрел бы я, кто из служащих посмеет меня критиковать!

BUREAUCRAT.—" They say I'm afraid of critics !   What rot !   I'd like to see any of them criticising me ! "

Reproduced from " Crocodile," by courtesy of " The New Leader "

PLATE 113   RALPH BARTON

"A TUESDAY NIGHT AT THE COCOANUT GROVE IN LOS ANGELES"

At Table No. 1, W. R. Hearst, Walter Wanger, Joseph M. Schenck, D. W. Griffith, William Fox, Louis B. Mayer, Cecil B. de Mille, Marcus Loew, Samuel Goldwyn, Carl Laemmle, Jesse Lasky, Adolph Zukor, Morris Gest, and the late arrival, Charlie Chaplin. *At Table No.* 2, Antonio Moreno, Carmel Myers, Conrad Nagel, Mabel Normand, Lew Cody, Mae Murray, Jim Cruze, Betty Compson. *At Table No.* 3, Wallace Beery, Colonel Tim McCoy, Hoot Gibson, Victor McLagen, Lon Chaney, Tom Mix, Noah Beery. *At Table No.* 4, Colleen, Tom, Owen and Matt Moore, May Allison, James R. Quirk, Lonella Parsons, Harold Lloyd. *At Table No.* 5, H. B. Warner, Corinne Griffith, Ramon Novarro, Edmund Goulding, Richard Dix. *At Table No.* 6, Max Reinhardt, Lya de Putti, Von Stroheim, Emil Jannings, Maurice Stiller, Vilma Banky, Lubitsch, Lil Dagovar, Lothar Mendes, F. W. Murnau, Joseph Schildkraut, Pola Negri. *At Table No.* 7, Aileen Pringle, Konrad Bercovici. H. L. Mencken, Anita Loos, George Jean Nathan, Paul Morand, Carl Van Vechten, Elinor Glyn,

By courtesy of the Editor of " Vanity Fair "

Joseph Hergesheimer, Theodore Dreiser, Jim Tully, Scott Fitzgerald. *At Table No.* 8, Buster Keaton, Bébé Daniels, Will Rogers, Lillian and Dorothy Gish, Constance and Norma Talmadge, Frances Marion. *At Table No.* 9, Ronald Colman, Beatrice Lillie, Bessie Love, George Fitzmaurice, Florence Vidor, Mary Philbin, Sid Grauman. *At Table No.* 10, Jack Dempsey, Estelle Taylor, Nazimova, Richard Barthelmess, Louise Brooks, Micky Neilan, Blanche Sweet. *At Table No.* 11, Syd Chaplin, Tom Meighan, Adolphe Menjou, Mack Sennett, Lionel Barrymore, Eddie Cantor, Harry Langdon, Renée Adorée. *At Table No.* 12, Anna Q. Nilsson, Clara Bow, Lowell Sherman, Justine Johnson, W. C. Fields. *At Table No.* 13, Irving Thalberg, Gloria Swanson, John Gilbert, Douglas Fairbanks, Mary Pickford, Greta Garbo, King Vidor, Pauline Starke, Norma Shearer, Jack Barrymore, Elinor Boardman, Marion Davies. *At Table No.* 14, Dolores Costello, Douglas Fairbanks, Jr., Betty Bronson, Billy Haines, Patsy Ruth Miller, Baby Peggy, Fanny Ward, Joan Crawford, Mary Astor, Sally O'Neil, Jackie Coogan, Lois Moran. The maître d'hotel, Will Hays

By courtesy of the Editor of " Vanity Fair "

PLATE 115   RALPH BARTON

Auguste Renoir painting more and more
broadly as time goes on

Paul Gauguin in Tahiti

Edgar Degas goes once too often
to the fount of his inspiration

Paul Cézanne, to prove that he has
the courage of his convictions,
devours his still-life

Edouard Manet in the pants
of his time (and of Goya's)

Pablo Picasso, beside himself

Henri Matisse, having made his own bed,
attempts to lie in it

MODERN ART

"LE PRESIDENT DE LA RÉPUBLIQUE"

From " Jean Cocteau : Dessins " (Librairie Stock)

PLATE 117

JEAN COCTEAU

"M. MILLERAND QUITTE TOULON"

From " Jean Cocteau : Dessins " (Librairie Stock)

PLATE 118   TOM TITT

GWEN FARRAR
By courtesy of the Editor of " The Sphere "

W. H. BERRY

By courtesy of the Editor of " Everybody's Weekly "

PLATE 120

LINE DRAWING FROM "NEGRO DRAWINGS"
By courtesy of Alfred A. Knopf, Limited

C. AUBREY SMITH AND JUNE WALKER IN "THE BACHELOR FATHER"

By courtesy of the Editor of "The New Yorker"

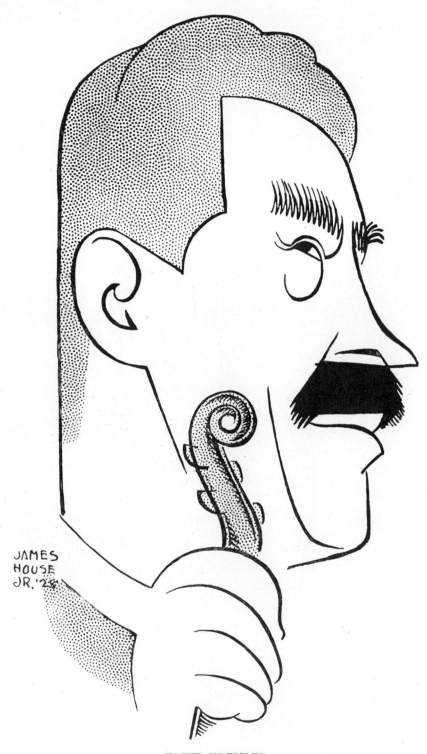

FRITZ KREISLER

By courtesy of the Editor of " The New Yorker "

PLATE 123   ALFRED FRUEH

WINIFRED LENIHAN IN "SAINT JOAN"

By courtesy of the Editor of "The New York World"

"OUR BETTERS"
Ina Claire and Constance Collier at the Henry Miller
By courtesy of the Editor of "The New Yorker"

President.
GENERAL MACHADO.

Secretary of State.
DR. MARTINEZ ORTIZ.

Secretary of Health.
DR. FERNANDEZ.

Secretary of War and Navy.
DR. ITURRALDE.

Secretary of the Treasury.
DR. GUTIERREZ DE CELIS.

Secretary of Justice.
DR. BARRAGUÉ.

Secretary of Agriculture.
GENERAL DELGADO.

Secretary of the President's Office.
DR. GUTIERREZ.

Secretary of Public Works.
DR. CESPEDES.

Secretary of the Interior.
COMANDANTE ZAYAS BAZAN.

Secretary of Public Instruction and Fine Arts.
GENERAL ALEMÁN.

Secretary of Communications.
DR. ABALLÍ.

"THE CUBAN CABINET"
Copyright (1928) Life Publishing Co.

PLATE 126   KARL ARNOLD

" ABENDEMPFANG "

" Die Deutsche Bank is doch prominent vertreten "
—" Na, dann hebt ja das kalte Büffett wieder den Kredit "

By courtesy of the Editor of " Simplicissimus "

"BRIDGE PROBLEM"

By courtesy of the Editor of "Judge"

PLATE 128   CHARLES MARTIN

" M. Koval est tour à tour la dominante fée du Printemps et le noceur
nostalgique "

By courtesy of the Editor of " femina "

"JULES RENARD"

From " Synthèses Littéraires et extra Littéraires " (Editions Mornay, Paris)

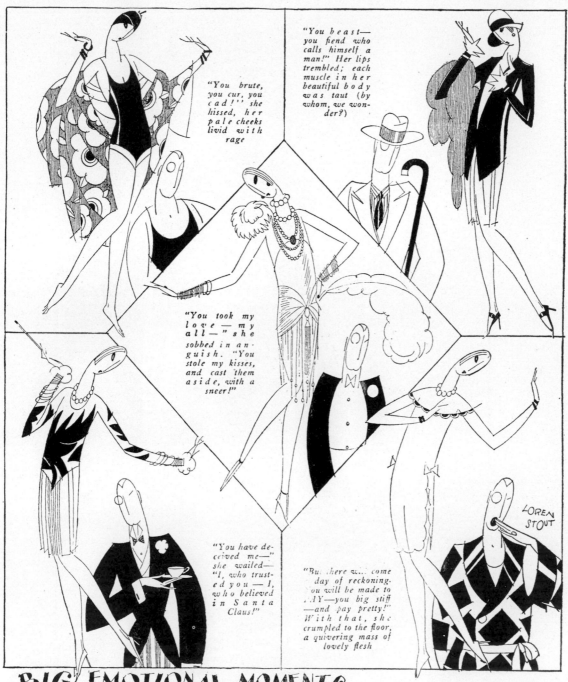

"You brute, you cur, you cad!'' she hissed, her pale cheeks livid with rage

"You beast— you fiend who calls himself a man!" Her lips trembled; each muscle in her beautiful body was taut (by whom, we wonder?)

"You took my love — my all—" she sobbed in anguish. "You stole my kisses, and cast them aside, with a sneer!"

"You have deceived me—" she wailed— "I, who trusted you — I, who believed in Santa Claus!"

"But there will come a day of reckoning. You will be made to PAY—you big stiff —and pay pretty!" With that, she crumpled to the floor, a quivering mass of lovely flesh

LOREN STOUT

BIG EMOTIONAL MOMENTS
WITH
THE FASHION MODEL

One of Those Girls Who Pose for Poiret Runs the Gamut in Ten Seconds—flat

PLATE 131

BIB

"LE FORGERON DE LA PAIX"

"C'est pour la paix que ce ' marteau travaille' . . . . ."

By courtesy of the Editor of "Le Charivari"

PLATE 132

KEIMEL

THE HIPPOPOTAMUS

PLATE 133

DUBOUT

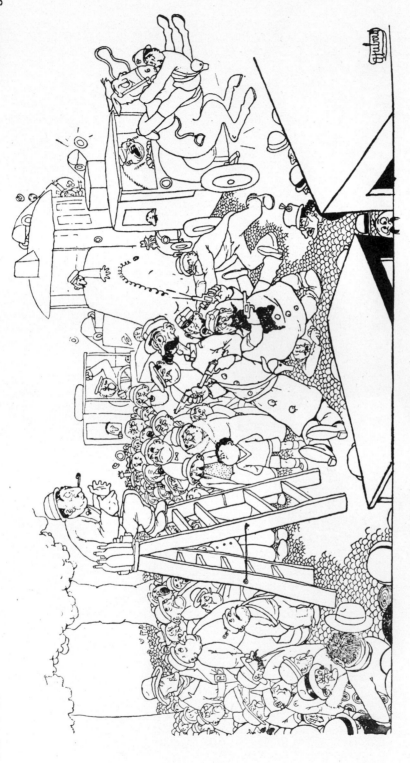

" De quoi ? Mais j'prends ma place pour voir la revue du 14 Juillet "

By courtesy of the Editor of " Le Rire "

PLATE 134　　　　　　　　　　WILLIAM GROPPER

"A RADICAL'S VIEW OF MUSSOLINI"
By courtesy of the Editor of "New Masses"

" The man who, twenty minutes before, had said, " Well, to make a long
story short . . . ."

Copyright (1928) *Life Publishing Co.*

PLATE 136

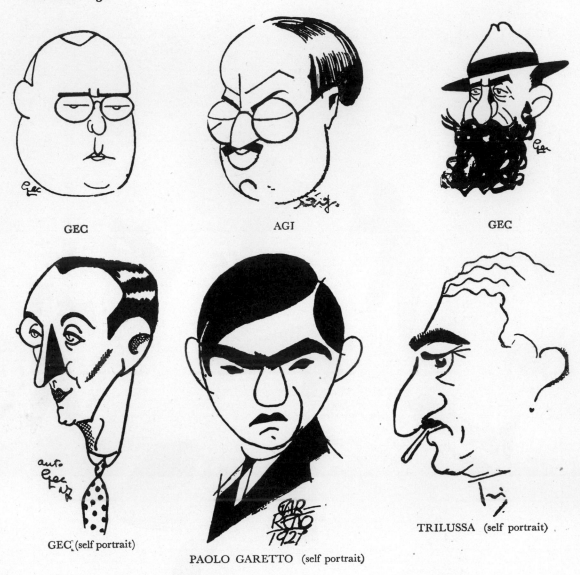

GEC   AGI   GEC

GEC (self portrait)

PAOLO GARETTO (self portrait)

TRILUSSA (self portrait)

GEC   GIRUS (self portrait)

IN THE PUBLIC EYE IN ITALY

By courtesy of the Editor of " Pasquino "